CELTIC RELIGION IN PRE-CHRISTIAN TIMES

By EDWARD ANWYL, M.A.

LATE CLASSICAL SCHOLAR OF ORIEL
COLLEGE, OXFORD PROFESSOR OF WELSH
AND COMPARATIVE PHILOLOGY AT THE
UNIVERSITY COLLEGE OF WALES,
ABERYSTWYTH ACTING-CHAIRMAN OF
THE CENTRAL WELSH BOARD FOR
INTERMEDIATE EDUCATION

Originally published in 1906.

FOREWORD

It is only as prehistoric archaeology has come to throw more and more light on the early civilizations of Celtic lands that it has become possible to interpret Celtic religion from a thoroughly modern viewpoint. The author cordially acknowledges his indebtedness to numerous writers on this subject, but his researches into some portions of the field especially have suggested to him the possibility of giving a new presentation to certain facts and groups of facts, which the existing evidence disclosed. It is to be hoped that a new interest in the religion of the Celts may thereby be aroused.

E. ANWYL.

ABERYSTWYTH, *February* 15, 1906.

CHAPTER I

--INTRODUCTORY: THE CELTS

In dealing with the subject of 'Celtic Religion' the first duty of the writer is to explain the sense in which the term 'Celtic' will be used in this work. It will be used in reference to those countries and districts which, in historic times, have been at one time or other mainly of Celtic speech. It does not follow that all the races which spoke a form of the Celtic tongue, a tongue of the Indo-European family, were all of the same stock. Indeed, ethnological and archaeological evidence tends to establish clearly that, in Gaul and Britain, for example, man had lived for ages before the introduction of any variety of Aryan or Indo-European speech, and this was probably the case throughout the whole of Western and Southern Europe. Further, in the light of comparative philology, it has now become abundantly clear that the forms of Indo-European speech which we call Celtic are most closely related to those of the Italic family, of which family Latin is the best known representative. From this it follows that we are to look for the centre of dissemination of Aryan Celtic speech in some district of Europe that could have been the natural centre of dissemination also for the Italic languages. From this common centre, through conquest and the commercial intercourse which followed it, the tribes which spoke the various forms of Celtic and Italic speech spread into the districts occupied by them in historic times. The common centre of radiation for Celtic and Italic speech was probably in the districts of Noricum and

Pannonia, the modern Carniola, Carinthia, etc., and the neighboring parts of the Danube valley. The conquering Aryan-speaking Celts and Italians formed a military aristocracy, and their success in extending the range of their languages was largely due to their skill in arms, combined, in all probability, with a talent for administration. This military aristocracy was of kindred type to that which carried Aryan speech into India and Persia, Armenia and Greece, not to speak of the original speakers of the Teutonic and Slavonic tongues. In view of the necessity of discovering a centre, whence the Indo-European or Aryan languages in general could have radiated Eastwards, as well as Westwards, the tendency to-day is to regard these tongues as having been spoken originally in some district between the Carpathians and the Steppes, in the form of kindred dialects of a common speech. Some branches of the tribes which spoke these dialects penetrated into Central Europe, doubtless along the Danube, and, from the Danube valley, extended their conquests together with their various forms of Aryan speech into Southern and Western Europe. The proportion of conquerors to conquered was not uniform in all the countries where they held sway, so that the amount of Aryan blood in their resultant population varied greatly. In most cases, the families of the original conquerors, by their skill in the art of war and a certain instinct of government, succeeded in making their own tongues the dominant media of communication in the lands where they ruled, with the result that most of the languages of Europe to-day are of the Aryan or Indo-European type. It does not, however, follow necessarily from this that the early religious ideas or the artistic civilization of countries now Aryan in speech, came necessarily from the conquerors rather than the conquered. In the last century it was long held that in countries of Aryan speech the essential features of their civilization, their religious ideas, their social institutions, nay, more, their inhabitants themselves, were of Aryan origin.

A more critical investigation has, however, enabled us to distinguish clearly between the development of various factors of human life which in their evolution can follow and often have followed more or less independent lines. The physical history of race, for instance, forms a problem by itself and must be studied by anthropological and ethnological methods. Language, again, has often spread along lines other than those of race, and its investigation appertains to the sphere of the philologist. Material civilisation, too, has not of necessity followed the lines either of racial or of linguistic development, and the search for its ancient trade-routes may be safely left to the archaeologist. Similarly the spread of ideas in religion and thought is one which has advanced on lines of its own, and its investigation must be conducted by the methods and along the lines of the comparative study of religions.

In the wide sense, then, in which the word 'Celtic religion' will be used in this work, it will cover the modes of religious thought prevalent in the countries and districts, which, in course of time, were mainly characterized by their Celtic speech. To the sum-total of these religious ideas contributions have been made from many sources. It would be rash to affirm that the various streams of

Aryan Celtic conquest made no contributions to the conceptions of life and of the world which the countries of their conquest came to hold (and the evidence of language points, indeed, to some such contributions), but their quota appears to be small compared with that of their predecessors; nor is this surprising, in view of the immense period during which the lands of their conquest had been previously occupied. Nothing is clearer than the marvelous persistence of traditional and immemorial modes of thought, even in the face of conquest and subjugation, and, whatever ideas on religion the Aryan conquerors of Celtic lands may have brought with them, they whose conquests were often only partial could not eradicate the inveterate beliefs of their predecessors, and the result in the end was doubtless some compromise, or else the victory of the earlier faith.

But the Aryan conquerors of Gaul and Italy themselves were not men who had advanced up the Danube in one generation. Those men of Aryan speech who poured into the Italian peninsula and into Gaul were doubtless in blood not unmixed with the older inhabitants of Central Europe, and had entered into the body of ideas which formed the religious beliefs of the men of the Danube valley. The common modifications of the Aryan tongue, by Italians and Celts alike, as compared with Greek, suggests contact with men of different speech. Among the names of Celtic gods, too, like those of other countries, we find roots that are apparently irreducible to any found in Indo-European speech, and we know not what pre-Aryan tongues may have contributed them. Scholars, to-day, are far more alive than they ever were before to the complexity of the contributory elements that have entered into the tissue of the ancient religions of mankind, and the more the relics of Celtic religion are investigated, the more complex do its contributory factors become. In the long ages before history there were unrecorded conquests and migrations innumerable, and ideas do not fail to spread because there is no historian to record them.

The more the scanty remnants of Celtic religion are examined, the clearer it becomes that many of its characteristic features had been evolved during the vast period of the ages of stone. During these millennia, men had evolved, concomitantly with their material civilization, a kind of working philosophy of life, traces of which are found in every land where this form of civilization has prevailed. Man's religion can never be dissociated from his social experience, and the painful stages through which man reached the agricultural life, for example, have left their indelible impress on the mind of man in Western Europe, as they have in every land. We are thus compelled, from the indications which we have of Celtic religion, in the names of its deities, its rites, and its survivals in folk-lore and legend, to come to the conclusion, that its fundamental groundwork is a body of ideas, similar to those of other lands, which were the natural correlatives of the phases of experience through which man passed in his emergence into civilized life. To demonstrate and to illustrate these relations will be the aim of the following chapters.

CHAPTER II

--THE CHIEF PHASES OF CELTIC
CIVILIZATION

In the chief countries of Celtic civilization, Gaul,
Cisalpine and Transalpine, Britain and Ireland,
abundant materials have been found for elucidating
the stages of culture through which man passed in
prehistoric times. In Britain, for example,
palaeolithic man has left numerous specimens of his
implements, but the forms even of these rude
implements suggest that they, too, have been
evolved from still more primitive types. Some
antiquarians have thought to detect such earlier
types in the stones that have been named 'eoliths'
found in Kent, but, though these 'eoliths' may
possibly show human use, the question of their
history is far from being settled. It is certain,
however, that man succeeded in maintaining
himself for ages in the company of the mammoth,
the cave-bear, and other animals now extinct.
Whether palaeolithic man survived the Ice Age in
Britain has not so far been satisfactorily decided. In
Gaul, however, there is fair evidence of continuity
between the Palaeolithic and Neolithic periods, and
this continuity must obviously have existed
somewhere. Still in spite of the indications of
continuity, the civilization of primitive man in Gaul
presents one aspect that is without any analogues in
the life of the palaeolithic men of the River Drift
period, or in that of man of the New Stone Age. The
feature in question is the remarkable artistic skill
shown by the cave men of the Dordogne district.
Some of the drawings and carvings of these men

reveal a sense of form which would have done credit to men of a far later age. A feature such as this, whatever may have been its object, whether it arose from an effort by means of 'sympathetic magic' to catch animals, as M. Salomon Reinach suggests, or to the mere artistic impulse, is a standing reminder to us of the scantiness of our data for estimating the lines of man's religious and other development in the vast epochs of prehistoric time.

We know that from the life of hunting man passed into the pastoral stage, having learned to tame animals. How he came to do so, and by what motives he was actuated, is still a mystery. It may be, as M. Salomon Reinach has also suggested, that it was some curious and indefinable sense of kinship with them that led him to do so, or more probably, as the present writer thinks, some sense of a need of the alliance of animals against hostile spirits. In all probability it was no motive which we can now fathom. The mind of early man was like the unfathomable mind of a boy. From the pastoral life again man passed after long ages into the life of agriculture, and the remains of neolithic man in Gaul and in Britain give us glimpses of his life as a farmer. The ox, the sheep, the pig, the goat, and the dog were his domestic animals; he could grow wheat and flax, and could supplement the produce of his farm by means of hunting and fishing. Neolithic man could spin and weave; he could obtain the necessary flint for his implements, which he made by chipping and polishing, and he could also make pottery of a rude variety. In its essentials we have here the beginnings of the agricultural civilization of man all the world over. In life, neolithic man dwelt sometimes in pit-dwellings and sometimes in hut-circles, covered with a roof of branches supported by a central pole. In death, he was buried with his kin in long mounds of earth called barrows, in chambered cairns and cromlechs or dolmens. The latter usually consist of three standing stones covered by a cap-stone; forming the stony skeleton of a grave that has been exposed to view after the mound of earth that covered it has been washed away. In their graves the dead were buried in a crouching attitude, and fresh burials were made as occasion required. Sometimes the cromlech is double, and occasionally there is a hole in one of the stones, the significance of which is unknown, unless it may have been for the ingress and egress of souls. Graves of the dolmen or cromlech type are found in all the countries of Western Europe, North Africa, and elsewhere, wherever stone suitable for the purpose abounds, and in this we have a striking illustration of the way in which lines of development in man's material civilization are sooner or later correlated to his geographical, geological, and other surroundings. The religious ideas of man in neolithic times also came into correlation with the conditions of his development, and the uninterpreted stone circles and pillars of the world are a standing witness to the religious zeal of a mind that was haunted by stone. Before proceeding to exemplify this thesis the subsequent trend of Celtic civilisation may be briefly sketched.

Through the pacific intercourse of commerce, bronze weapons and implements began to find their way, about 2000 B.C. or earlier, from Central and

Southern Europe into Gaul, and thence into Britain. In Britain the Bronze Age begins at about 1500 or 1400 B.C., and it is thought by some archaeologists that bronze was worked at this period by the aid of native tin in Britain itself. There are indications, however, that the introduction of bronze into Britain was not by way of commerce alone. About the beginning of the Bronze period are found evidences in this island of a race of different type from that of neolithic man, being characterised by a round skull and a powerful build, and by general indications of a martial bearing. The remains of this race are usually found in round barrows.

This race, which certainly used bronze weapons, is generally believed to have been the first wave that reached Britain of Aryan conquerors of Celtic speech from the nearest part of the continent, where it must have arrived some time previously, probably along the Rhine valley. As the type of Celtic speech that has penetrated farthest to the west is that known as the Goidelic or Irish, it has not unreasonably been thought that this must have been the type that arrived in Britain first. There are indications, too, that it was this type that penetrated furthest into the west of Gaul. Its most marked characteristic is its preservation of the pronunciation of U as 'oo' and of QU, while the 'Brythonic' or Welsh variety changed U to a sound pronounced like the French 'u' or the German 'u' and also QU to P. There is a similar line of cleavage in the Italic languages, where Latin corresponds to Goidelic, and Oscan and Umbrian to Brythonic. Transalpine Gaul was probably invaded by Aryan-speaking Celts from more than one direction, and the infiltration and invasion of new- comers, when it had once begun, was doubtless continuous through these various channels. There are cogent reasons for thinking that ultimately the dominant type of Celtic speech over the greater part of Gaul came to be that of the P rather than the QU type, owing to the influx from the East and Northeast of an overflow from the Rhine valley of tribes speaking that dialect; a dialect which, by force of conquest and culture, tended to spread farther and farther West. Into Britain, too, as time went on, the P type of Celtic was carried, and has survived in Welsh and Cornish, the remnants of the tongue of ancient Britain. We know, too, from the name Eporedia (Yvrea), that this dialect of Celtic must have spread into Cisalpine Gaul. The latter district may have received its first Celtic invaders direct from the Danube valley, as M. Alexandre Bertrand held, but it would be rash to assume that all its invaders came from that direction. In connection, however, with the history of Celtic religion it is not the spread of the varying types of Celtic dialect that is important, but the changes in the civilization of Gaul and Britain, which reacted on religious ideas or which introduced new factors into the religious development of these lands.

The predatory expeditions and wars of conquest of military Celtic tribes in search for new homes for their superfluous populations brought into prominence the deities of war, as was the case also with the ancient Romans, themselves an agricultural and at the same time a predatory race. The prominence of war in Celtic tribal life at one stage has left us the names of a large number of deities that were identified with Mars and Bellona, though all the war-gods were not originally such. In the Roman calendar there is abundant evidence that Mars was at one time an agricultural god as well as a god of war. The same, as will be shown later, was the probable history of some of the Celtic deities, who were identified in Roman times with Mars and Bellona. Caesar tells us that Mars had at one time been the chief god of the Gauls, and that in Germany that was still the case. In Britain, also, we find that there were several deities identified with Mars, notably Belatucadrus and Cocidius, and this, too, points in the direction of a development of religion under military influence. The Gauls appear to have made great strides in military matters and in material civilisation during the Iron Age. The culture of the Early Iron Age of Hallstatt had been developed in Gaul on characteristic lines of its own, resulting in the form now known as the La Tene or Marnian type. This type derives it name from the striking specimens of it that were discovered at La Tene on the shore of Lake Neuchatel, and in the extensive cemeteries of the Marne valley, the burials of which cover a period of from 350-200 B.C. It was during the third century B.C. that this characteristic culture of Gaul reached its zenith, and gave definite shape to the beautiful curved designs known as those of Late-Celtic Art. Iron appears to have been introduced into Britain about 300 B.C., and the designs of Late-Celtic Art are here represented best of all. Excellent specimens of Late-Celtic culture have been found in Yorkshire and elsewhere, and important links with continental developments have been discovered at Aylesford, Aesica, Limavady, and other places. Into the development of this typical Gaulish culture elements are believed to have entered by way of the important commercial avenue of the Rhone valley from Massilia (Marseilles), from Greece (*via* Venetia), and possibly from Etruria. Prehistoric archaeology affords abundant proofs that, in countries of Celtic speech, metal-working in bronze, iron, and gold reached a remarkably high pitch of perfection, and this is a clear indication that Celtic countries and districts which were on the line of trade routes, like the Rhone valley, had attained to a material civilisation of no mean character before the Roman conquest. In Britain, too, the districts that were in touch with continental commerce had, as Caesar tells us, also developed in the same direction. The religious counterpart of this development in civilization is the growth in many parts of Gaul, as attested by Caesar and by many inscriptions and place-names, of the worship of gods identified with Mercury and Minerva, the deities of civilization and commerce. It is no accident that one of the districts most conspicuous for this worship was the territory of the Allobrogic confederation, where the commerce of the Rhone valley found its most remarkable development. From this sketch of Celtic civilization it will readily be seen how here as elsewhere the religious development of the Celts stood closely related to the development of their civilization generally. It must be borne in mind, however, that all parts of the Celtic world were not equally affected by the material development in question. Part of the complexity of the history of Celtic religion arises from the fact that we cannot be always certain of the degree of progress in civilization which any given district had made, of the ideas which pervaded it, or of the absorbing interests of its life. Another difficulty, too, is that the accounts of Celtic religion given by ancient authorities do not always harmonies with the indisputable evidence of inscriptions. The probability is that the religious practices of the Celtic world were no more homogeneous than its general civilization, and that the ancient authorities are substantially true in their statements about certain districts, certain periods, or certain sections of society, while the inscriptions, springing as they do from the influence of the Gallo-Roman civilisation, especially of Eastern Gaul and military Britain, give us most valuable supplementary evidence for districts and environments of a different kind. The inscriptions, especially by the names of deities which they reveal, have afforded most valuable clues to the history of Celtic religion, even in stages of civilisation earlier than those to which they themselves belong. In the next chapter the correlation of Celtic religious ideas to the stages of Celtic civilisation will be further developed.

CHAPTER III

--THE CORRELATION OF CELTIC RELIGION
WITH THE GROWTH OF CELTIC
CIVILIZATION

In dealing with the long vista of prehistoric time, it
is very difficult for us, in our effort after
perspective, not to shorten unduly in our thoughts
the vast epochs of its duration. We tend, too, to
forget, that in these unnumbered millennia there
was ample time for it to be possible over certain
areas of Europe to evolve what were practically
new races, through the prepotency of particular
stocks and the annihilation of others. During these
epochs, again, after speech had arisen, there was
time enough to recast completely many a language,
for before the dawn of history language was no
more free from change than it is now, and in these
immense epochs whatever ideas as to the world of
their surroundings were vaguely felt by prehistoric
men and formulated for them by their kinsmen of
genius, had abundant time in which to die or to win
supremacy. There must have been aeons before the
dawn even of conscious animism, and the
experiment of trying sympathetic magic was, when
first attempted, probably regarded as a master-
stroke of genius. The Stone Age itself was a long
era of great if slow progress in civilization, and the
evolution of the practices and ideas which emerge
as the concomitants of its agricultural stage, when
closely regarded, bear testimony to the mind's
capacity for religious progress in the light of
experience and intelligent experiment, and at the
same time to the errors into which it fell. The Stone

Age has left its sediment in all the folk-lore of the
world. To the casual observer many of the ideas
embedded in it may seem a mass of error, and so
they are when judged unhistorically, but when
viewed critically, and at the same time historically,
they afford many glimpses of prehistoric genius in a
world where life was of necessity a great
experiment. The folk-lore of the world reveals for
the same stages of civilization a wonderful
uniformity and homogeneity, as Dr. J. G. Frazer has
abundantly shown in his *Golden Bough*. This
uniformity is not, however, due to necessary
uniformity of origin, but to a great extent to the fact
that it represents the state of equilibrium arrived at
between minds at a certain level and their
environment, along lines of thought directed by the
momentum given by the traditions of millennia, and
the survival in history of the men who carefully
regarded them. The apparently unreasoned
prohibitions often known as 'taboos,' many of which
still persist even in modern civilized life, have their
roots in ideas and experiences which no speculation
of ours can now completely fathom, however much
we may guess at their origin. Many of these ancient
prohibitions have vanished under new conditions,
others have often survived from a real or supposed
harmony with new experiences, that have arisen in
the course of man's history. After passing through a
stage when he was too preoccupied with his
material cares and wants to consider whether he
was haunted or not, early man in the Celtic world as
elsewhere, after long epochs of vague unrest, came
to realize that he was somehow haunted in the
daytime as well as at night, and it was this sense of
being haunted that impelled his intellect and his

imagination to seek some explanation of his feelings. Primitive man came to seek a solution not of the Universe as a whole (for of this he had no conception), but of the local Universe, in which he played a part. In dealing with Celtic folk-lore, it is very remarkable how it mirrors the characteristic local coloring and scenery of the districts in which it has originated. In a country like Wales, for example, it is the folk-lore of springs, caves, mountains, lakes, islands, and the forms of its imagination, here as elsewhere, reflect unmistakably the land of its origin. Where it depicts an 'other world,' that 'other world' is either on an island or it is a land beneath the sea, a lake, or a river, or it is approachable only through some cave or opening in the earth. In the hunting-grounds of the Celtic world the primitive hunter knew every cranny of the greater part of his environment with the accuracy born of long familiarity, but there were some peaks which he could not scale, some caves which he could not penetrate, some jungles into which he could not enter, and in these he knew not what monsters might lurk or unknown beings might live. In Celtic folk-lore the belief in fabulous monsters has not yet ceased. Man was surrounded by dangers visible and invisible, and the time came when some prehistoric man of genius propounded the view that all the objects around him were no less living than himself. This animistic view of the world, once adopted, made great headway from the various centres where it originated, and man derived from it a new sense of kinship with his world, but also new terrors from it. Knowing from the experience of dreams that he himself seemed able to wander away from himself, he thought in course of time that other living things were somehow double, and the world around him came to be occupied, not merely with things that were alive, but with other selves of these things, that could remain in them or leave them at will. Here, again, this new prehistoric philosophy gave an added interest to life, but it was none the less a source of fresh terrors. The world swarmed with invisible spirits, some friendly, some hostile, and, in view of these beings, life had to be regulated by strict rules of actions and prohibitions. Even in the neolithic stage the inhabitants of Celtic countries had attained to the religious ideas in question, as is seen not only by their folk-lore and by the names of groups of goddesses such as the Matres (or mothers), but by the fact that in historic times they had advanced well beyond this stage to that of named and individualized gods. As in all countries where the gods were individualized, the men of Celtic lands, whether aborigines or invaders, had toiled along the steep ascent from the primitive vague sense of being haunted to a belief in gods who, like Esus, Teutates, Grannos, Bormanus, Litavis, had names of a definite character.

Among the prohibitions which had established themselves among the races of Celtic lands, as elsewhere, was that directed against the shedding of the blood of one's own kin. There are indications, too, that some at any rate of the tribes inhabiting these countries reckoned kinship through the mother, as in fact continued to be the case among the Picts of Scotland into historic times. It does not follow, as we know from other countries, that the pre-Aryan tribes of Gaul and Britain, or indeed the

Aryan tribes themselves in their earliest stage, regarded their original ancestors as human. Certain names of deities such as Tarvos (the bull), Moccos (the pig), Epona (the goddess of horses), Damona (the goddess of cattle), Mullo (the ass), as well as the fact that the ancient Britons, according to Caesar, preserved the hen, the goose, and the hare, but did not kill and eat them, all point to the fact that in these countries as elsewhere certain animals were held in supreme respect and were carefully guarded from harm. Judging from the analogy of kindred phenomena in other countries, the practice of respecting certain animals was often associated with the belief that all the members of certain clans were descended from one or other of them, but how far this system was elaborated in the Celtic world it is hard to say. This phenomenon, which is widely known as totemism, appears to be suggested by the prominence given to the wild boar on Celtic coins and ensigns, and by the place assigned on some inscriptions and bas-reliefs to the figure of a horned snake as well as by the effigies of other animals that have been discovered. It is not easy to explain the beginnings of totemism in Gaul or elsewhere, but it should always be borne in mind that early man could not regard it as an axiomatic truth that he was the superior of every other animal. To reach that proud consciousness is a very high step in the development of the human perspective, and it is to the credit of the Celts that, when we know them in historic times, they appear to have attained to this height, inasmuch as the human form is given to their deities. It is not always remembered how great a step in religious evolution is implied when the gods are clothed with human attributes. M. Salomon

Reinach, in his account of the vestiges of totemism among the Celts, suggests that totemism was merely the hypertrophy of early man's social sense, which extended from man to the animals around him. This may possibly be the case, but it is not improbable that man also thought to discover in certain animals much-needed allies against some of the visible and invisible enemies that beset him. In his conflict with the malign powers around him, he might well have regarded certain animals as being in some respects stronger combatants against those powers than himself; and where they were not physically stronger, some of them, like the snake, had a cunning and a subtlety that seemed far to surpass his own. In course of time certain bodies of men came to regard themselves as being in special alliance with some one animal, and as being descended from that animal as their common ancestor. The existence side by side of various tribes, each with its definite totem, has not yet been fully proved for the Gaulish system, and may well have been a developed social arrangement that was not an essential part of such a mode of thought in its primary forms. The place of animal-worship in the Celtic religion will be more fully considered in a later chapter. Here it is only indicated as a necessary stage in relation to man's civilization in the hunting and the pastoral stages, which had to be passed through before the historic deities of Gaul and Britain in Roman times could have come into being. Certain of the divine names of the historic period, like Artio (the bear-goddess), Moccus (the pig), Epona (the mare), and Damona (the sheep), bear the unmistakable impress of having been at one time those of animals.

As for the stage of civilization at which totemism originated, there is much difference of opinion. The stage of mind which it implies would suggest that it reflects a time when man's mind was preoccupied with wild beasts, and when the alliances and friendships, which he would value in life, might be found in that sphere. There is much plausibility in the view put forward by M. Salomon Reinach, that the domestication of animals itself implies a totemistic habit of thought, and the consequent protection of these animals by means of taboos from harm and death. It may well be that, after all, the usefulness of domestic animals from a material point of view was only a secondary consideration for man, and a happy discovery after unsuccessful totemistic attentions to other animals. We know not how many creatures early man tried to associate with himself but failed.

In all stages of man's history the alternation of the seasons must have brought some rudiments of order and system into his thoughts, though for a long time he was too preoccupied to reflect upon the regularly recurring vicissitudes of his life. In the pastoral stage, the sense of order came to be more marked than in that of hunting, and quickened the mind to fresh thought. The earth came to be regarded as the Mother from whom all things came, and there are abundant indications that the earth as the Mother, the Queen, the Long-lived one, etc., found her natural place as a goddess among the Celts. Her names and titles were probably not in all places or in all tribes the same. But it is in the agricultural stage that she entered in Celtic lands, as she did in other countries, into her completest religious heritage, and this aspect of Celtic religion will be dealt with more fully in connection with the spirits of vegetation. This phase of religion in Celtic countries is one which appears to underlie some of its most characteristic forms, and the one which has survived longest in Celtic folk-lore. The Earth-mother with her progeny of spirits, of springs, rivers, mountains, forests, trees, and corn, appears to have supplied most of the grouped and individualized gods of the Celtic pantheon. The Dis, of whom Caesar speaks as the ancient god of the Gauls, was probably regarded as her son, to whom the dead returned in death. Whether he is the Gaulish god depicted with a hammer, or as a huge dog swallowing the dead, has not yet been established with any degree of certainty.

CHAPTER IV

--CELTIC RELIGION AND THE DEVELOPMENT OF INDIVIDUALIZED DEITIES

Like other religions, those of the Celtic lands of Europe supplemented the earlier animism by a belief in spirits, who belonged to trees, animals, rocks, mountains, springs, rivers, and other natural phenomena, and in folk-lore there still survives abundant evidence that the Celt regarded spirits as taking upon themselves a variety of forms, animal and human. It was this idea of spirits in animal form that helped to preserve the memory of the older totemism into historic times. It is thus that we have names of the type of Brannogenos (son of the raven), Artogenos (son of the bear), and the like, not to speak of simpler names like Bran (raven), March (horse), surviving into historic times. Bronze images, too, have been found at Neuvy-en-Sullias, of a horse and a stag (now in the Orleans museum), provided with rings, which were, as M. Salomon Reinach suggests, probably used for the purpose of carrying these images in procession. The wild boar, too, was a favourite emblem of Gaul, and there is extant a bronze figure of a Celtic Diana riding on a boar's back. At Bolar, near Nuits, there was discovered a bronze mule. In the museum at Mayence is a bas-relief of the goddess of horses, Epona (from the Gaulish *Epos*=Lat. *equus*, horse), riding on horseback. One of the most important monuments of this kind is a figure of Artio, the bear-goddess (from Celtic *Artos*, a bear), found at Muri near Berne. In front of her stood a figure of a bear, which was also found with her. The bull of the Tarvos Trigaranos bas-relief of Notre Dame was also in all likelihood originally a totem, and similarly the horned serpents of other bas-reliefs, as well as the boar found on Gaulish ensigns and coins, especially in Belgic territory. There is a representation, too, of a raven on a bas-relief at Compiegne. The name 'Moccus,' which is identified with Mercury, on inscriptions, and which is found inscribed at Langres, Trobaso, the valley of the Ossola and the Borgo san Dalmazzo, is undoubtedly the philological equivalent of the Welsh *moch* (swine). In Britain, too, the boar is frequently found on the coins of the Iceni and other tribes. In Italy, according to Mr. Warde Fowler, the pig was an appropriate offering to deities of the earth, so that in the widespread use of the pig as a symbol in the Celtic world, there may be some ancient echo of a connection between it and the earth-spirit. Its diet of acorns, too, may have marked it out, in the early days of life in forest- clearings, as the animal embodiment of the oak-spirit. In the legends of the Celtic races, even in historic times, the pig, and especially the boar, finds an honored place. In addition to the animals aforementioned, the ass, too, was probably at one time venerated in one of the districts of Gaul, and it is not improbable that Mullo, the name of a god identified with Mars and regarded as the patron of muleteers, mentioned on inscriptions (at Nantes, Craon, and Les Provencheres near Craon), meant originally 'an ass.' The goddess Epona, also, whose worship was widely spread, was probably at one time an animal goddess in the form of a mare, and the name of another goddess, Damona, either from the root *dam*=Ir. *dam*, (ox); or Welsh *daf-ad* (sheep), may similarly be that of an ancient totem sheep or cow. Nor was it in the animal world alone that the Celts saw indications of the divine. While the chase and the pastoral life concentrated the mind's attention on the life of animals, the growth of agriculture fixed man's thoughts on the life of the earth, and all that grew upon it, while at the same time he was led to think more and more of the mysterious world beneath the earth, from which all things came and to which all things returned. Nor could he forget the trees of the forest, especially those which, like the oak, had provided him with their fruit as food in time of need. The name Druid, as well as that of the centre of worship of the Gauls of Asia Minor, Drunemeton (the oak-grove), the statement of Maximus of Tyre that the representation of Zeus to the Celts was a high oak, Pliny's account of Druidism (*Nat. Hist.*, xvi. 95), the numerous inscriptions to Silvanus and Silvana, the mention of Dervones or Dervonnae on an inscription at Cavalzesio near Brescia, and the abundant evidence of survivals in folk- lore as collected by Dr. J. G. Frazer and others, all point to the fact that tree-worship, and especially that of the oak, had contributed its full share to the development of Celtic religion, at any rate in some districts and in some epochs. The development of martial and commercial civilization in later times tended to restrict its typical and more primitive developments to the more conservative parts of the Celtic world. The fact that in Caesar's time its main centre in Gaul was in the territory of the Carnutes, the tribe which has given its name to Chartres, suggests that its chief votaries were mainly in that part of the country. This, too, was the district of the god Esus (the eponymous god of the Essuvii), and in some degree of Teutates, the cruelty of whose rites is mentioned by Lucan. It had occurred to the present writer, before finding the same view expressed by M. Salomon Reinach, that the worship of Esus in Gaul was almost entirely local in character. With regard to the rites of the Druids, Caesar tells us that it was customary to make huge images of wickerwork, into which human beings, usually criminals, were placed and burnt. The use of wickerwork, and the suggestion that the rite was for purifying the land, indicates a combination of the ideas of tree-worship with those of early agricultural life. When the Emperor Claudius is said by Suetonius to have suppressed Druidism, what is meant is, in all probability, that the more inhuman rites were suppressed, leading, as the Scholiasts on Lucan seem to suggest, to a substitution of animal victims for men. On the side of civil administration and education, the functions of the Druids, as the successors of the primitive medicine men and magicians, doubtless varied greatly in different parts of Gaul and Britain according to the progress that had been made in the differentiation of functions in social life. The more we investigate the state of the Celtic world in ancient times, the clearer it becomes, that in civilization it was very far from being homogeneous, and this heterogeneity of civilization must have had its influence on religion as well as on other social phenomena. The natural conservatism of agricultural life, too, perpetuated many practices even into comparatively late times, and of these we catch a glimpse in Gregory of Tours, when he tells us that at Autun the goddess

Berecyntia was worshiped, her image being carried on a wagon for the protection of the fields and the vines. It is not impossible that by Berecyntia Gregory means the goddess Brigindu, whose name occurs on an inscription at Volnay in the same district of Gaul. The belief in corn-spirits, and other ideas connected with the central thought of the farmer's life, show, by their persistence in Celtic as well as other folklore, how deeply they had entered into the inner tissue of the agricultural mind, so as to be linked to its keenest emotions. Here the rites of religion, whether persuasive as in prayer, or compulsory as in sympathetic magic, whether associated with communal or propitiatory sacrifice, whether directed to the earth or to the heaven, all had an intensely practical and terribly real character, due to man's constant preoccupation with the growth and storage of food for man and beast. In the hunting, the pastoral, and above all in the agricultural life, religion was not a matter merely of imagination or sentiment, but one most intimately associated with the daily practice of life, and this practical interest included in its purview rivers, springs, forests, mountains, and all the setting of man's existence. And what is true of agriculture is true also, in a greater or less degree, of the life of the Celtic metal-worker or the Celtic sailor. Even in late Welsh legend Amaethon (old Celtic *Ambactonos*), the patron god of farming (Welsh *Amaeth*), and Gofannon, the patron god of the metal-worker (Welsh *gof*, Irish *gobha*), were not quite forgotten, and the prominence of the worship of the counterparts of Mercury and Minerva in Gaul in historic times was due to the sense of respect and gratitude, which each trade and each locality felt for the deity who had rid the land of monsters, and who had brought man into the comparative calm of civilized life.

CHAPTER V

--THE HUMANIZED GODS OF CELTIC RELIGION

One of the most striking facts connected with the Celtic religion is the large number of names of deities which it includes. These names are known to us almost entirely from inscriptions, for the most part votive tablets, in acknowledgment of some benefit, usually that of health, conferred by the god on man. In Britain these votive tablets are chiefly found in the neighborhood of the Roman walls and camps, but we cannot be always certain that the deities mentioned are indigenous. In Gaul, however, we are on surer ground in associating certain deities with certain districts, inasmuch as the evidence of place-names is often a guide. These inscriptions are very unevenly distributed over Gaulish territory, the Western and the North-Western districts being very sparsely represented.

In the present brief sketch it is impossible to enter into a full discussion of the relations of the names found on inscriptions to particular localities, and the light thus thrown on Celtic religion; but it may be here stated that investigation tends to confirm the local character of most of the deities which the inscriptions name. Out of these deities, some, it is true, in the process of evolution, gained a wider field of worshipers, while others, like Lugus, may even have been at one time more widely worshipped than they came to be in later times. Occasionally a name like Lugus (Irish *Lug*), Segomo (Irish, in the genitive, *Segamonas*), Camulos, whence Camulodunum (Colchester), Belenos (Welsh *Belyn*), Maponos (Welsh *Mabon*), Litavis (Welsh *Llydaw*), by its existence in Britain as well as in Gaul, suggests that it was either one of the ancient deities of the Aryan Celts, or one whose worship came to extend over a larger area than its fellows. Apart from a few exceptional considerations of this kind, however, the local character of the deities is most marked.

A very considerable number are the deities of springs and rivers. In Noricum, for example, we have Adsalluta, a goddess associated with Savus (the river Save). In Britain 'the goddess' Deva (the Dee), and Belisama (either the Ribble or the Mersey), a name meaning 'the most warlike goddess,' are of this type. We have again Axona the goddess of the river Aisne, Sequana, the goddess of the Seine, Ritona of the river Rieu, numerous nymphs and many other deities of fountains. Doubtless many other names of local deities are of this kind. Aerial phenomena appear to have left very few clear traces on the names of Celtic deities. Vintios, a god identified with Mars, was probably a god of the wind, Taranucus, a god of thunder, Leucetios, a god of lightning, Sulis (of Bath) a sun-goddess, but beyond these there are few, if any, reflections of the phenomena of the heavens. Of the gods named on inscriptions nearly all are identified with Mercury, Mars, or Apollo. The gods who came to be regarded as culture-deities appear from their names to be of various origins: some are humanized totems, others are in origin deities of vegetation or local natural phenomena. As already indicated, it is clear that the growth of commercial and civilized life in certain districts had brought into prominence deities identified with Mercury and Minerva as the patrons of civilization. Military men, especially in Britain, appear to have favored deities like Belatucadros (the brilliant in war), identified with Mars.

About fourteen inscriptions mentioning him have been found in the North of England and the South of Scotland. The goddess Brigantia (the patron-deity of the Brigantes), too, is mentioned on four inscriptions: Cocidius, identified with Mars, is mentioned on thirteen: while another popular god appears to have been Silvanus. Among the most noticeable names of the Celtic gods identified with Mercury are Adsmerius or Atesmerius, Dumiatis (the god of the Puy de Dome), Iovantucarus (the lover of youth), Teutates (the god of the people), Caletos (the hard), and Moccus (the boar). Several deities are identified with Mars, and of these some of the most noticeable names are Albiorix (world-king), Caturix (battle-king), Dunatis (the god of the fort), Belatucadrus (the brilliant in war), Leucetius (the god of lightning), Mullo (the mule), Ollovidius (the all-knowing) Vintius (the wind-god), and Vitucadrus (the brilliant in energy). The large number of names identified with Mars reflects the prominent place at one time given to war in the ideas that affected the growth of the religion of the Celtic tribes. Of the gods identified with Hercules, the most interesting name is Ogmios (the god of the furrow) given by Lucian, but not found on any inscription. The following gods too, among others, are identified with Jupiter: Aramo (the gentle), Ambisagrus (the persistent), Bussumarus (the large-lipped), Taranucus (the thunderer), Uxellimus (the highest). It would seem from this that in historic times at any rate Jupiter did not play a large part in Celtic religious ideas.

There remains another striking feature of Celtic religion which has not yet been mentioned, namely the identification of several deities with Apollo. These deities are essentially the presiding deities of certain healing-springs and health-resorts, and the growth of their worship into popularity is a further striking index to the development of religion side by side with certain aspects of civilization. One of the names of a Celtic Apollo is Borvo (whence Bourbon), the deity of certain hot springs. This name is Indo-European, and was given to the local fountain- god by the Celtic-speaking invaders of Gaul: it simply means 'the Boiler.' Other forms of the name are also found, as Bormo and Bormanus. At Aquae Granni (Aix-la-Chapelle) and elsewhere the name identified with Apollo is Grannos. We find also Mogons, and Mogounus, the patron deity of Moguntiacum (Mainz), and, once or twice, Maponos (the great youth). The essential feature of the Apollo worship was its association in Gallo-Roman civilization with the idea of healing, an idea which, through the revival of the worship of AEsculapius, affected religious views very strongly in other quarters of the empire. It was in this conception of the gods as the guides of civilization and the restorers of health, that Celtic religion, in some districts at any rate, shows itself emerging into a measure of light after a long and toilsome progress from the darkness of prehistoric ideas. What Caesar says of the practice of the Gauls of beginning the year with the night rather than with the day, and their ancient belief that they were sprung from Dis, the god of the lower world, is thus typified in their religious history.

In dealing with the deities of the Celtic world we must not, however, forget the goddesses, though their history presents several problems of great difficulty. Of these goddesses some are known to us by groups--Proximae (the kinswomen), Dervonnae (the oak-spirits), Niskai (the water-sprites), Mairae, Matronae, Matres or Matrae (the mothers), Quadriviae (the goddesses of cross roads). The Matres, Matrae, and Matronae are often qualified by some local name. Deities of this type appear to have been popular in Britain, in the neighborhood of Cologne and in Provence. In some cases it is uncertain whether some of these grouped goddesses are Celtic or Teutonic. It is an interesting parallel to the existence of these grouped goddesses, when we find that in some parts of Wales 'Y Mamau' (the mothers) is the name for the fairies. These grouped goddesses take us back to one of the most interesting stages in the early Celtic religion, when the earth-spirits or the corn-spirits had not yet been completely individualized. Of the individualized goddesses many are strictly local, being the names of springs or rivers. Others, again, appear to have emerged into greater individual prominence, and of these we find several associated on inscriptions, sometimes with a god of Celtic name, but sometimes with his Latin counterpart. It is by no means certain that the names so linked together were thus associated in early times, and the fashion may have been a later one, which, like other fashions, spread after it had once begun. The relationship in some cases may have been regarded as that of mother and son, in others that of brother and sister, in others that of husband and wife, the data are not adequate for the final decision of the question. Of these associated pairs the following may be noted, Mercurius and Rosmerta, Mercurius and Dirona, Grannus (Apollo) and Sirona, Sucellus and Nantosvelta, Borvo and Damona, Cicolluis (Mars) and Litavis, Bormanus and Bormana, Savus and Adsalluta, Mars and Nemetona. One of these names, Sirona, probably meant the long-lived one, and was applied to the earth-mother. In Welsh one or two names have survived which, by their structure, appear to have been ancient names of goddesses; these are Rhiannon (Rigantona, the great queen), and Modron (Matrona, the great mother). The other British deities will be more fully treated by another writer in this series in a work on the ancient mythology of the British Isles. It is enough to say that research tends more and more to confirm the view that the key to the history of the Celtic deities is the realization of the local character of the vast majority of them.

CHAPTER VI

--THE CELTIC PRIESTHOOD

No name in connection with Celtic religion is more
familiar to the average reader than that of the
Druids, yet there is no section of the history of
Celtic religion that has given rise to greater
discussion than that relating to this order. Even the
association of the name with the Indo-European
root *dru-*, which we find in the Greek word *drus*, an
oak, has been questioned by such a competent
Celtic scholar as M. d'Arbois de Jubainville, but on
this point it cannot be said that his criticism is
conclusive. The writers of the ancient world who
refer to the Druids, do not always make it
sufficiently clear in what districts the rites,
ceremonies, and functions which they were
describing prevailed. Nor was it so much the
priestly character of the Druids that produced the
deepest impression on the ancients. To some
philosophical and theological writers of antiquity
their doctrines and their apparent affinities with
Pythagoreanism were of much greater interest than
their ceremonial or other functions. One thing at
any rate is clear, that the Druids and their doctrines,
or supposed doctrines, had made a deep impression
on the writers of the ancient world. There is a
reference to them in a fragment of Aristotle (which
may not, however, be genuine) that is of interest as
assigning them a place in express terms both among
the Celts and the Galatae. The prominent feature of
their teaching which had attracted the attention of
other writers, such as the historian Diodorus Siculus
and the Christian theologian Clement of Alexandria,

was the resemblance of their doctrine concerning the immortality and transmigration of the soul to the views of Pythagoras. Ancient writers, however, did not always remember that a religious or philosophical doctrine must not be treated as a thing apart, but must be interpreted in its whole context in relation to its development in history and in the social life of the community in which it has flourished. To some of the ancients the superficial resemblance between the Druidic doctrine of the soul's future and the teaching attributed to Pythagoras was the essential point, and this was enough to give the Druids a reputation for philosophy, so that a writer like Clement of Alexandria goes so far as to regard the Druids of the 'Galatae' along with the prophets of the Egyptians, the 'Chaldaeans' of the Assyrians, the 'philosophers of the Celts,' and the Magi of the Persians as the pioneers of philosophy among the barbarians before it spread to the Greeks. The reason for the distinction drawn in this passage between the 'Druids of the Galatae' and 'the philosophers of the Celts' is not clear. Diodorus Siculus calls attention to the Druidic doctrine that the souls of men were immortal, and that after the lapse of an appointed number of years they came to life again, the soul then entering into another body. He says that there were certain 'philosophers and theologians' that were called Druids who were held in exceptional honour. In addition to these, the Celts, he says, had also seers, who foretold the future from the flight of birds and by means of the offering of sacrifices. According to him it was these priestly seers who had the masses in subjection to them. In great affairs they had, he says, the practice of divination by the slaughter of a human victim, and the observation of the attitude in which he fell, the contortions of the limbs, the spurting of the blood, and the like. This, he states, was an ancient and established practice. Moreover, it was the custom, according to Diodorus, to make no sacrifice without the presence of a philosopher (apparently a Druid in addition to the sacrificing seer), the theory being that those who were authorities on the divine nature were to the gods intelligible mediators for the offering of gifts and the presentation of petitions. These philosophers were in great request, together with their poets, in war as well as in peace, and were consulted not merely by the men of their own side, but also by those of the enemy. Even when two armies were on the point of joining battle, these philosophers had been able, Diodorus says, to step into the space between them and to stop them from fighting, exactly as if they had charmed wild beasts. The moral which Diodorus draws from this is, that even among the wildest of barbarians the spirited principle of the soul yields to wisdom, and that Ares (the god of war) even there respects the Muses. It is clear from this account that Diodorus had in mind the three classes of non-military professional men among the Celts, to whom other ancient writers also refer, namely, the Bards, the Seers, and the Druids. His narrative is apparently an expansion, in the light of his reading and philosophical meditation, of information supplied by previous writers, notably Posidonius. The latter, too, appears to have been Julius Caesar's chief authority, in addition to his own observation, but Caesar does not appear expressly to indicate the triple division here in question. The account which he gives is important,

and would be even more valuable than it is had he
told us how far what he describes was written from
his own personal information, and the degree of
variation (if any) of religious practice in different
districts. However, Caesar's statements deserve the
closest consideration. After calling attention to the
division of the Gaulish aristocracy into two main
sections, the Druids and the Knights, he proceeds to
speak of the Druids. These were occupied, he says,
with religious matters, they attended to public and
private sacrifices, and interpreted omens. Moreover,
they were the teachers of the country. To them the
young men congregated for knowledge, and the
pupils held their teachers in great respect. They,
too, were the judges in public and private disputes:
it was they who awarded damages and penalties.
Any contumacy in reference to their judgments was
punished by exclusion from the sacrifices. This
sentence of excommunication was the severest
punishment among the Gauls. The men so punished
were treated as outlaws, and cut off from all human
society, with its rights and privileges. Over these
Druids there was one head, who wielded the highest
influence among them. On his death the nearest of
the others in dignity succeeded him, or, if several
were equal, the election of a successor was made by
the vote of the Druids. Sometimes the primacy was
not decided without the arbitrament of arms. The
Druids met at a fixed time of the year in a
consecrated spot in the territory of the Carnutes, the
district which was regarded as being in the centre of
the whole of Gaul. This assembly of Druids formed
a court for the decision of cases brought to them
from everywhere around. It was thought, Caesar
says, that the doctrine of the Druids was discovered

in Britain and thence carried over into Gaul. At that
time, too, those who wanted to make a profounder
study of it resorted thither for their training. The
Druids had immunity from military service and
from the payment of tribute. These privileges drew
many into training for the profession, some of their
own accord, others at the instance of parents and
relatives. While in training they were said to learn
by heart a large number of verses, and some went so
far as to spend twenty years in their course of
preparation. The Druids held it wrong to put their
religious teaching in writing, though, in almost
everything else, whether public or private affairs,
they made use of Greek letters. Caesar thought that
they discouraged writing on the one hand, lest their
teaching should become public property; on the
other, lest reliance upon writing should lessen the
cultivation of the memory. To this risk Caesar could
testify from his own knowledge. Their cardinal
doctrine was that souls did not perish, but that after
death they passed from one person to another; and
this they regarded as a supreme incentive to valour,
since, with the prospect of immortality, the fear of
death counted for nothing. They carried on,
moreover, many discussions about the stars and
their motion, the greatness of the universe and the
lands, the nature of things, the strength and power
of the immortal gods, and communicated their
knowledge to their pupils. In another passage
Caesar says that the Gauls as a people were
extremely devoted to religious ideas and practices.
Men who were seriously ill, who were engaged in
war, or who stood in any peril, offered, or promised
to offer, human sacrifices, and made use of the
Druids as their agents for such sacrifices. Their

theory was, that the immortal gods could not be appeased unless a human life were given for a human life. In addition to these private sacrifices, they had also similar human sacrifices of a public character. Caesar further contrasts the Germans with the Gauls, saying that the former had no Druids to preside over matters of religion, and that they paid no attention to sacrifices.

In his work on divination, Cicero, too, refers to the profession which the Druids made of natural science, and of the power of foretelling the future, and instances the case of the AEduan Diviciacus, his brother's guest and friend. Nothing is here said by Cicero of the three classes implied in Diodorus, but Timagenes (quoted in Ammianus) refers to the three classes under the names 'bardi,' 'euhages' (a mistake for 'vates'), and 'drasidae' (a mistake for 'druidae'). The study of nature and of the heavens is here attributed to the second class of seers (vates). The highest class, that of the Druids, were, he says, in accordance with the rule of Pythagoras, closely linked together in confraternities, and by acquiring a certain loftiness of mind from their investigations into things that were hidden and exalted, they despised human affairs and declared the soul immortal. We see here the view expressed that socially as well as intellectually the Druids lived according to the Pythagorean philosophy. Origen also refers to the view that was prevalent in his time, that Zamolxis, the servant of Pythagoras, had taught the Druids the philosophy of Pythagoras. He further states that the Druids practised sorcery. The triple division of the non-military aristocracy is perhaps best given by Strabo, the Greek geographer, who here follows Posidonius. The three classes are the Bards, the Seers (ouateis=vates), and Druids. The Bards were hymn-writers and poets, the Seers sacrificers and men of science, while the Druids, in addition to natural science, practiced also moral philosophy. They were regarded as the justest of men, and on this account were intrusted with the settlement of private and public disputes. They had been the means of preventing armies from fighting when on the very verge of battle, and were especially intrusted with the judgment of cases involving human life. According to Strabo, they and their fellow-countrymen held that souls and the universe were immortal, but that fire and water would sometime prevail. Sacrifices were never made, Strabo says, without the intervention of the Druids. Pomponius Mela says that in his time (c. 44 A.D.), though the ancient savagery was no more, and the Gauls abstained from human sacrifices, some traces of their former practices still remained, notably in their habit of cutting a portion of the flesh of those condemned to death after bringing them to the altars. The Gauls, he says, in spite of their traces of barbarism, had an eloquence of their own, and had the Druids as their teachers in philosophy. These professed to know the size and form of the earth and of the universe, the motions of the sky and stars, and the will of the gods. He refers, as Caesar does, to their work in education, and says that it was carried on in caves or in secluded groves. Mela speaks of their doctrine of immortality, but says nothing as to the entry of souls into other bodies. As a proof of this belief he speaks of the practice of burning and burying with the dead things appropriate to the needs of the living. Lucan, the Latin poet, in his *Pharsalia*, refers to the seclusion of the Druids' groves and to their doctrine of immortality. The Scholiasts' notes on this passage are after the manner of their kind, and add very little to our knowledge. In Pliny's *Natural History* (xvi, 249), however, we seem to be face to face with another, though perhaps a distorted, tradition. Pliny was an indefatigable compiler, and appears partly by reading, partly by personal observation, to have noticed phases of Celtic religious practices which other writers had overlooked. In the first place he calls attention to the veneration in which the Gauls held the mistletoe and the tree on which it grew, provided that that tree was the oak. Hence their predilection for oak groves and their requirement of oak leaves for all religious rites. Pliny here remarks on the consonance of this practice with the etymology of the name Druid as interpreted even through Greek (the Greek for an oak being *drus*). Were not this respect for the oak and for the mistletoe paralleled by numerous examples of tree and plant-worship given by Dr. Frazer and others, it might well have been suspected that Pliny was here quoting some writer who had tried to argue from the etymology of the name Druid. Another suspicious circumstance in Pliny's account is his reference to the serpent's egg composed of snakes rolled together into a ball. He states that he himself had seen such an 'egg,' of about the size of an apple. Pliny, too, states that Tiberius Caesar abolished by a decree of the Senate the Druids and the kind of seers and physicians the Gauls then had. This statement, when read in its context, probably refers to the prohibition of human sacrifices. The historian Suetonius, in his account of the Emperor Claudius, also states that Augustus had prohibited 'the religion of the Druids' (which, he says, 'was one of fearful savagery') to Roman citizens, but that Claudius had entirely abolished it. What is here also meant, in view of the description given of Druidism, is doubtless the abolishing of its human sacrifices. In later Latin writers there are several references to Druidesses, but these were probably only sorceresses. In Irish the name *drui* (genitive *druad*) meant a magician, and the word *derwydd* in mediaeval Welsh was especially used in reference to the vaticinations which were then popular in Wales.

When we analyse the testimony of ancient writers concerning the Druids, we see in the first place that to different minds the name connoted different things. To Caesar it is the general name for the non-military professional class, whether priests, seers, teachers, lawyers, or judges. To others the Druids are pre-eminently the philosophers and teachers of the Gauls, and are distinguished from the seers designated *vates*. To others again, such as Pliny, they were the priests of the oak-ritual, whence their name was derived. In view of the variety of grades of civilization then co-existing in Gaul and Britain, it is not improbable that the development of the non-military professional class varied very considerably in different districts, and that all the aspects of Druidism which the ancient writers specify found their appropriate places in the social system of the Celts. In Gaul and Britain, as elsewhere, the office of the primitive tribal medicine-man was capable of indefinite development, and all the forms of its evolution could not have proceeded *pari passu* where the sociological conditions found such scope for variation. It may well be that the oak and mistletoe ceremonies, for example, lingered in remote agricultural districts long after they had ceased to interest men along the main routes of Celtic civilisation. The bucolic mind does not readily abandon the practices of millennia.

In addition to the term Druid, we find in Aulus Hirtius' continuation of Caesar's *Gallic War* (Bk. viii., c. xxxviii., 2), as well as on two inscriptions, one at Le-Puy-en-Velay (Dep. Haute-Loire), and the other at Macon (Dep. Saone-et-Loire), another priestly title, 'gutuater.' At Macon the office is that of a 'gutuater Martis,' but of its special features nothing is known.

CHAPTER VII

--THE CELTIC OTHER-WORLD

In the preceding chapter we have seen that the belief was widely prevalent among Greek and Roman writers that the Druids taught the immortality of the soul. Some of these writers, too,

point out the undoubted fact, attested by
Archaeology, that objects which would be
serviceable to the living were buried with the dead,
and this was regarded as a confirmation of the view
that the immortality of souls was to the Celts an
object of belief. The study of Archaeology on the
one hand, and of Comparative Religion on the
other, certainly leads to the conclusion that in the
Bronze and the Early Iron Age, and in all
probability in the Stone Age, the idea prevailed that
death was not the end of man. The holed cromlechs
of the later Stone Age were probably designed for
the egress and ingress of souls. The food and the
weapons that were buried with the dead were
thought to be objects of genuine need. Roman
religion, too, in some of its rites provided means for
the periodical expulsion of hungry and hostile
spirits of the dead, and for their pacification by the
offer of food. A tomb and its adjuncts were meant
not merely for the honour of the dead, but also for
the protection of the living. A clear line of
distinction was drawn between satisfied and
beneficent ghosts like the Manes, and the
unsatisfied and hostile ghosts like the Lemures and
Larvae. To the Celtic mind, when its analytical
powers had come to birth, and man was sufficiently
self-conscious to reflect upon himself, the problem
of his own nature pressed for some solution. In
these solutions the breath, the blood, the name, the
head, and even the hair generally played a part, but
these would not in themselves explain the
mysterious phenomena of sleep, of dreams, of
epilepsy, of madness, of disease, of man's shadow
and his reflection, and of man's death. By long
familiarity with the scientific or quasi-scientific

explanations of these things, we find it difficult to realize fully their constant fascination for early man, who had his thinkers and philosophies like ourselves. One very widely accepted solution of early man in the Celtic world was, that within him there was another self which could live a life of its own apart from the body, and which survived even death, burial, and burning. Sometimes this inner self was associated with the breath, whence, for example, the Latin 'anima' and the Welsh 'enaid,' both meaning the soul, from the root *an-*, to breathe. At other times the term employed for the second self had reference to man's shadow: the Greek 'skia,' the Latin 'umbra,' the Welsh 'ysgawd,' the English 'shade.' There are abundant evidences, too, that the life-principle was frequently regarded as being especially associated with the blood. Another tendency, of which Principal Rhys has given numerous examples in his Welsh folk-lore, was to regard the soul as capable of taking a visible form, not necessarily human, preferably that of some winged creature. In ancient writers there is no information as to the views prevalent among the Celts regarding the forms or the abodes of the spirits of the dead, beyond the statement that the Druids taught the doctrine of their re-birth. We are thus compelled to look to the evidence afforded by myth, legend, and folk-lore. These give fair indications as to the types of earlier popular belief in these matters, but it would be a mistake to assume that the ideas embodied in them had remained entirely unchanged from remote times. The mind of man at certain levels is quite capable of evolving new myths and fresh folk-lore along the lines of its own psychology and its own logic. The forms which the soul could take doubtless varied greatly in men's opinions in different districts and in different mental perspectives, but folk-lore tends to confirm the view that early man, in the Celtic world as elsewhere, tended to emphasis his conception of the subtlety and mobility of the soul as contrasted with the body. Sooner or later the primitive philosopher was bound to consider whither the soul went in dreams or in death. He may not at first have thought of any other sphere than that of his own normal life, but other questions, such as the home of the spirits of vegetation in or under the earth, would suggest, even if this thought had not occurred to him before, that the spirits of men, too, had entrance to the world below. Whether this world was further pictured in imagination depended largely on the poetic genius of any given people. The folk-lore of the Celtic races bears abundant testimony to their belief that beneath this world there was another. The 'annwfn' of the Welsh was distinctly conceived in the folk-lore embodied in mediaeval poetry as being 'is elfydd' (beneath the world). In mediaeval Welsh legend, again, this lower world is regarded as divided into kingdoms, like this world, and its kings, like Arawn and Hafgan in the Mabinogi of Pwyll, are represented as being sometimes engaged in conflict. From this lower world had come to man some of the blessings of civilisation, and among them the much prized gift of swine. The lower world could be even plundered by enterprising heroes. Marriages like that of Pwyll and Rhiannon were possible between the dwellers of the one world and the other. The other-world of the Celts does not seem, however, to have been always pictured as beneath the earth. Irish and Welsh legend combine in viewing it at times as situated on distant islands, and Welsh folk-lore contains several suggestions of another world situated beneath the waters of a lake, a river, or a sea. In one or two passages also of Welsh mediaeval poetry the shades are represented as wandering in the woods of Caledonia (Coed Celyddon). This was no doubt a traditional idea in those families that migrated to Wales in post- Roman times from Strathclyde. To those who puzzled over the fate of the souls of the dead the idea of their re-birth was a very natural solution, and Mr. Alfred Nutt, in his *Voyage of Bran*, has called attention to the occurrence of this idea in Irish legend. It does not follow, however, that the souls of all men would enjoy the privilege of this re-birth. As Mr. Alfred Nutt points out, Irish legend seems to regard this re-birth only as the privilege of the truly great. It is of interest to note the curious persistence of similar ideas as to death and the other-world in literature written even in Christian times and by monastic scribes. In Welsh, in addition to Annwfn, a term which seems to mean the 'Not-world,' we have other names for the world below, such as 'anghar,' the loveless place; 'difant,' the unrimmed place (whence the modern Welsh word 'difancoll,' lost for ever); 'affwys,' the abyss; 'affan,' the land invisible. The upper-world is sometimes called 'elfydd,' sometimes 'adfant,' the latter term meaning the place whose rim is turned back. Apparently it implies a picture of the earth as a disc, whose rim or lip is curved back so as to prevent men from falling over into the 'difant,' or the rimless place. In modern Celtic folk-lore the various local other- worlds are the abodes of fairies, and in these traditions there may possibly be, as

Principal Rhys has suggested, some intermixture of reminiscences of the earlier inhabitants of the various districts. Modern folk-lore, like mediaeval legend, has its stories of the inter-marriages of natives of this world with those of the other-world, often located underneath a lake. The curious reader will find several examples of such stories in Principal Rhys's collection of Welsh and Manx folk-lore. In Irish legend one of the most classical of these stories is that of the betrothal of Etain, a story which has several points of contact with the narrative of the meeting of Pwyll and Rhiannon in the Welsh Mabinogi. The name of Arthur's wife, Gwenhwyfar, which means 'the White Spectre,' also suggests that originally she too played a part in a story of the same kind. In all these and similar narratives, it is important to note the way in which the Celtic conceptions of the other-world, in Britain and in Ireland, have been colored by the geographical aspects of these two countries, by their seas, their islands, their caves, their mounds, their lakes, and their mountains. The local other-worlds of these lands bear, as we might have expected, the clear impress of their origin. On the whole the conceptions of the other-world which we meet in Celtic legend are joyous; it is a land of youth and beauty. Cuchulainn, the Irish hero, for example, is brought in a boat to an exceedingly fair island round which there is a silver wall and a bronze palisade. In one Welsh legend the cauldron of the Head of Annwfn has around it a rim of pearls. One Irish story has a naive description of the glories of the Celtic Elysium in the words--'Admirable was that land: there are three trees there always bearing fruit, one pig always alive, and another ready cooked.'

Occasionally, however, we find a different picture. In the Welsh poem called 'Y Gododin' the poet Aneirin is represented as expressing his gratitude at being rescued by the son of Llywarch Hen from 'the cruel prison of the earth, from the abode of death, from the loveless land.' The salient features, therefore, of the Celtic conceptions of the other-world are their consonance with the suggestions made by Celtic scenery to the Celtic imagination, the vagueness and variability of these conceptions in different minds and in different moods, the absence of any ethical considerations beyond the incentive given to bravery by the thought of immortality, and the remarkable development of a sense of possible inter-relations between the two worlds, whether pacific or hostile. Such conceptions, as we see from Celtic legend, proved an admirable stimulus and provided excellent material for the development of Celtic narrative, and the weird and romantic effect was further heightened by the general belief in the possibilities of magic and metamorphosis. Moreover, the association with innumerable place-names of legends of this type gave the beautiful scenery of Celtic lands an added charm, which has attached their inhabitants to them with a subtle and unconquerable attachment scarcely intelligible to the more prosaic inhabitants of prosaic lands. To the poetic Celt the love of country tends to become almost a religion. The Celtic mind cannot remain indifferent to lands and seas whose very beauty compels the eyes of man to gaze upon them to their very horizon, and the lines of observation thus drawn to the horizon are for the Celt continual temptations to the thought of an infinity beyond.

The preoccupation of the Celtic mind with the deities of his scenery, his springs, his rivers, his seas, his forests, his mountains, his lakes, was in thorough keeping with the tenor of his mind, when tuned to its natural surroundings. In dealing with Celtic religion, mythology, and legend, it is not so much the varying local and temporal forms that demand our attention, as the all-pervading and animating spirit, which shows its essential character even through the scanty remains of the ancient Celtic world. Celtic religion bears the impress of nature on earth far more than nature in the heavens. The sense of the heaven above has perhaps survived in some of the general Indo-European Celtic terms for the divine principle, and there are some traces of a religious interest in the sun and the god of thunder and lightning, but every student of Celtic religion must feel that the main and characteristic elements are associated with the earth in all the variety of its local phenomena. The great earth-mother and her varied offspring ever come to view in Celtic religion under many names, and the features even of the other-world could not be dissociated for the Celt from those of his mother-earth. The festivals of his year, too, were associated with the decay and the renewal of her annual life. The bonfires of November, May, Midsummer, and August were doubtless meant to be associated with the vicissitudes of her life and the spirits that were her children. For the Celt the year began in November, so that its second half-year commenced with the first of May. The idea to which Caesar refers, that the Gauls believed themselves descended from Dis, the god of the lower world, and began the year with the night, counting their time not by days but by nights, points in the same direction, namely that the darkness of the earth had a greater hold on the mind than the brightness of the sky. The Welsh terms for a week and a fortnight, *wythnos* (eight nights) and *pythefnos* (fifteen nights) respectively confirm Caesar's statement. To us now it may seem more natural to associate religion with the contemplation of the heavens, but for the Celtic lands at any rate the main trend of the evidence is to show that the religious mind was mainly drawn to a contemplation of the earth and her varied life, and that the Celt looked for his other-world either beneath the earth, with her rivers, lakes, and seas, or in the islands on the distant horizon, where earth and sky met. This predominance of the earth in religion was in thorough keeping with the intensity of religion as a factor in his daily pursuits. It was this intensity that gave the Druids at some time or other in the history of the Western Celts the power which Caesar and others assign to them. The whole people of the Gauls, even with their military aristocracy, were extremely devoted to religious ideas, though these led to the inhumanity of human sacrifices. At one time their sense of the reality of the other-world was so great, that they believed that loans contracted in this world would be repaid there, and practical belief could not go much further than that. All these considerations tend to show how important it is, in the comparative study of religions, to investigate each religion in its whole sociological and geographical environment as well as in the etymological meaning of its terms.

In conclusion, the writer hopes that this brief sketch, which is based on an independent study of the main evidence for the religious ideas and practices of the Celtic peoples, will help to interest students of religion in the dominant modes of thought which from time immemorial held sway in these lands of the West of Europe, and which in folk-lore and custom occasionally show themselves even in the midst of our highly developed and complex civilization of to-day. The thought of early man on the problems of his being--for after all his superstitions reveal thought--deserve respect, for in his efforts to think he was trying to grope towards the light.

SHORT BIBLIOGRAPHY

RHYS, *Hibbert Lectures on Celtic Heathendom.*

RHYS, *Celtic Folk-lore, Welsh and Manx.*

REINACH, S., *Cultes, Mythes et Religion.*

NUTT, ALFRED, *The Voyage of Bran.*

SQUIRE, *Mythology of the British Islands.*

GAIDOZ, *Esqiusse de Mythologie gauloise.*

BERTRAND, *La Religion des Gaulois, les Druides et le Druidisme.*

FRAZER, *The Golden Bough.*

JOYCE, *The Social History of Ireland.*

D'ARBOIS DE JUBAINVILLE, *Les Druides et les dieux celtiques a forme d'animaux.*

WINDISCH, *Irische Texte mit Worterbuch.*

CYNDDELW, *Cymru Fu.*

FOULKES, *Enwogion Cymru.*

CAMPBELL, *Popular Tales of the West Highlands.*

Made in the USA
Middletown, DE
15 February 2021